Nelson Gr International

Pupil Book 6

Series Edi

Nelson Tho

Published in 2011 by:
Nelson Thornes Ltd
Delta Place
27 Bath Road
CHELTENHAM
GL53 7TH
United Kingdom

11 12 13 14 15 / 10 9 8 7 6 5 4 3 2 1

A catalogue record for this book is available from the British Library

ISBN 978 1 4085 0858 9

Illustrations by Andrew Peters and Alan Rogers

Page make-up by The OKS Group

Printed by Multivista Global Ltd

Contents

We can use a single **adjective** to describe a noun.

An **old** woman is crossing the road.
'Old' is a single adjective.

We can use an **adjective phrase** to describe a noun.

An old woman **with a big, floppy hat** is crossing the road.
'With a big, floppy hat' is an adjective phrase.
Joining two adjectives makes an adjective phrase.

The garden, **silent and deserted**, was covered in snow.
'Silent and deserted' is an adjective phrase.

> **TIP**
> A **phrase** is a group of words that does not have a main verb.

Focus

A How would you describe these?

1 your friend   ------------------ and ------------------
2 your house   ------------------ and ------------------
3 a river with   ------------------

B Copy the sentences. Underline the **adjective phrase**.

1 The weather, cold and wet, lasted all week.
2 Five small blue flowers grew by the side of the road.
3 The boy with the old, heavy school bag walked slowly.
4 The children, tired but happy, fell asleep.

Practice

A Use the **adjective phrases** in sentences of your own.

1 kind and helpful
2 with no shoes
3 frozen and slippery
4 with loud cries
5 old but useful
6 without an umbrella

B Write a sentence with an adjective phrase to describe each of these nouns.

1 field
2 feathers
3 cough
4 tiger
5 farmer
6 photograph

Extension

Three of the examples below are **adjective phrases**.
Three of the examples below are sentences.

1 thank you said Jim
2 Janet ran home
3 shivering and frightened
4 give me that
5 with a torn jacket
6 seven gold and red flags

A Find the three adjective phrases.
Add a verb and any other words you need to make each one into a sentence.

B Find the three sentences.
Write them with the correct punctuation.

Letters added to the front of a word are called **prefixes**.
Some prefixes can change a word so that it means the opposite.

Prefix	Examples			
un	happy	**un**happy	wise	**un**wise
in	visible	**in**visible	sane	**in**sane
im	possible	**im**possible	patient	**im**patient
dis	appear	**dis**appear	trust	**dis**trust
il	legal	**il**legal	legible	**il**legible
anti	clockwise	**anti**clockwise	climax	**anti**climax

Prefixes have special meanings.
Here are some more common prefixes and their meanings.

Prefix	Meaning	Examples	
bi	two	**bi**cycle	**bi**lingual
ex	out of	**ex**port	**ex**it
inter	between	**inter**val	**inter**national
mis	wrong	**mis**behave	**mis**judge
re	again	**re**place	**re**turn
sub	under	**sub**marine	**sub**way

Focus

A Make the opposite of these words by adding a **prefix**.

1 true

2 loyal

3 moveable

4 secure

5 honour

6 pure

7 well

8 mobile

9 approve

10 logical

11 agree

12 active

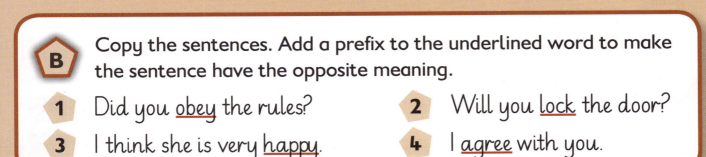

B Copy the sentences. Add a prefix to the underlined word to make the sentence have the opposite meaning.

1 Did you <u>obey</u> the rules?

2 Will you <u>lock</u> the door?

3 I think she is very <u>happy</u>.

4 I <u>agree</u> with you.

Practice

A Match each of the words in the box with its correct meaning.

rewrite   incapable   invisible
disbelieve   recommence

TIP
Use a dictionary to help you.

1 to begin again

2 not able to be seen

3 not able to do something

4 to think that something is not true

5 to put words on paper again

B Use each of the words in the box in a sentence of your own.

Extension

A Use a dictionary to find one word that begins with each of these **prefixes**.

1 inter   **2** bi   **3** pro   **4** pre   **5** mono

6 sub   **7** post   **8** auto   **9** al   **10** re

B Put each word that you found in **A** into a sentence of your own.

C Use a dictionary to help you write the meaning of these words.

1 explosion   **2** extension   **3** invasion   **4** biped

5 preparation   **6** submerge   **7** mistake   **8** revise

TIP
Auxiliary verbs are helper verbs.

Sometimes we need more than one **verb** to help a sentence work properly.

We need to use an **auxiliary verb** to help the main verb. The verb 'to be' is often used as an auxiliary verb.

He **was** teaching me how to do this.
He **is** teaching me how to do this.
He **will** teach me how to do this.

Here are some more auxiliary verbs.

has	She **has** gone out.
have	I **have** forgotten my book.
had	We **had** seen the fox many times.
must	You **must** clean your room.
might	I **might** catch the early train.
could	I **could** meet you at twelve o'clock.
should	You **should** wear a helmet when you ride your bike.
would	They **would** enjoy swimming today.

Focus

A Say what the **auxiliary verb** in each sentence is.

1 We have finished.

2 They will arrive early.

3 You must finish soon.

4 He would like an ice cream.

5 I might feel better soon.

B Copy the sentences. Underline the auxiliary verb in each sentence.

1 I would like a new bicycle.

2 I must leave at six o'clock.

3 The telephone has rung seven times.

4 I could find the station on the map.

Practice

Copy the sentences. Use the **auxiliary verbs** in the box to fill the gaps.

1 Flowers _____ growing in the field last year.

2 I _____ putting butter on my bread before I put on the jam.

3 She _____ going to visit her aunt.

4 We _____ hoping to finish this before we go.

5 He _____ playing football when he hurt his hand.

am
are
is
was
were

Extension

A These sentences are written in the **present continuous tense**. Change the two **auxiliary verbs** in each sentence so they are in the **past continuous tense**.

1 I am thinking about what I am going to do.

2 We are walking to town and then we are going to catch a bus.

3 They are wondering what they are going to find.

B These sentences are written in the past continuous tense. Change the auxiliary verb and the **main verb** so that each sentence is in the **future tense**.

1 I was meeting a friend at three o'clock.

2 We were running for the bus.

A **pronoun** can be used instead of a noun.

Noun	Pronoun
The horse is in the field.	**It** is in the field.

Some pronouns show ownership or possession. These are called **possessive pronouns**.

This coat is **mine** and that coat is **yours**.

Here are some more possessive pronouns.

Possessive pronoun	Example	Meaning
mine	The red bicycle is **mine**.	belongs to me
yours	Is this **yours**?	belongs to you
his	The book on the floor is **his**.	belongs to him
hers	This new book is **hers**.	belongs to her
its	The baby has **its** hat on.	belongs to it
ours	All the sheep in that field are **ours**.	belongs to us
theirs	Our garden is bigger than **theirs**.	belongs to them

Focus

A Say what the **possessive pronoun** for each sentence is.

1 I have a hamster. The hamster is _____.

2 He has a football. The football is _____.

3 We have a cousin. The cousin is _____.

4 You have a secret. The secret is _____.

5 They have a car. The car is _____.

B Copy the sentences.
Use possessive pronouns in place of the underlined words.

1 Your writing is neater than <u>my writing</u>.

2 She has lost her pencil. Is this <u>her pencil</u>?

3 That pond is smaller than <u>our pond</u>.

4 Are those <u>their books</u> on the desk?

Practice

Copy the sentences. Write a **possessive pronoun** in each gap.

1 "This chair is _____ and that chair is _____,"
said John to his sister.

2 "These scarves are _____," shouted the boys.

3 Sam made a cake. Lynn helped him, so it is _____
as well.

4 The children had to take some baby photographs to school.
The twins were not sure they could find _____.

5 The teacher asked for the homework. Katy and I hadn't
brought _____.

Extension

Write a sentence using each pair of **possessive pronouns**, like this:
This book is <u>mine</u> and that book is <u>yours</u>.

1 mine   yours

2 theirs   ours

3 his   hers

4 ours   his

5 hers   mine

TIP

A **suffix** is an ending.

Nouns can be made from **verbs**, usually by adding a suffix like 'ing', 'er' or 'ment'.

Verb	Nouns	
to paint	the paint**ing**	the paint**er**
to manage	the manage**ment**	the manag**er**

But be careful! Sometimes the word changes when a noun is made from a verb.

Verb	Nouns	
to thieve	the thie**f**	the th**eft**

Focus

A Say your answers to these questions.

1 A person who explores is an _____.

2 A person who writes is a _____.

3 A person who farms is a _____.

4 A person who teaches is a _____.

5 A person who paints is a _____.

6 A person who swims is a _____.

B Copy the list of **verbs** in the box on the left.
Next to each verb, write the matching **noun** from the box on the right.

to sing	to laugh	to explore
to run	to drive	to explain
to lose	to build	to argue

runner	singer	explanation
building	loser	exploration
laughter	driver	argument

Practice

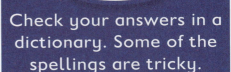

TIP
Check your answers in a dictionary. Some of the spellings are tricky.

Copy the sentences.
Make a **noun** from the **verb** in brackets to fill the gap in each sentence.

1   Amy made a good (to suggest).

2   The (to enter) to the cave was blocked by rocks.

3   The Big Book of (to know) was helpful for my project.

6   The old house needed many (to improve).

5   David had an (to injure) after the race.

6   Sally was a very good (to ride).

Extension

A   Look up each of these **nouns** in your dictionary. Write the **verb** from which it is made.

1   conversation   2   embarrassment

3   alteration   4   imagination

5   invention   6   decision

7   agreement   8   permission

9   invitation   10 punishment

B   Choose four of the nouns from A and use them in sentences of your own.

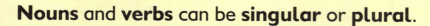

Nouns and **verbs** can be **singular** or **plural**.

When we use a singular noun we must use a singular verb.

The **tunnel goes** under the sea.

singular noun   **singular verb**

When we use a **plural noun** we must use a **plural verb**.

The **cockerels crow** in the morning.

plural noun   **plural verb**

The words 'each' and 'every' always come before singular nouns.

Each flower **has** colourful petals.
Every petal **is** very delicate.

Collective nouns are always followed by a singular verb.

The **herd lives** on the hill.
The **flock** of birds **flies** overhead.

Sums of money and popular food are singular.

The price of the magazine **is $5**.
Fish and chips is not a healthy meal.

Focus

A Say if these **nouns** and **verbs** are **singular** or **plural**.

1 The boy laughs.

2 The girls run.

3 Every day is wet and cold.

4 The bunch of flowers is dead.

5 Pizza is easy to cook.

6 The choir sings beautifully.

B Copy these **nouns** into your book. Write whether each would be followed by a singular or a plural verb.

1 the sandals   2 80 cents   3 each boy

4 eggs on toast   5 this group   6 every horse

Practice

Copy the sentences. Choose the **singular** or **plural verb** to complete each one.

1 We is/are careful about locking the door.
2 The group play/plays on Saturdays.
3 Each ticket has/have a number on it.
4 Curry and rice is/are my favourite meal.
5 Horses trot/trots and gallop/gallops.

Extension

A Add a **predicate** to each of these subjects to make a sentence.

1 The orchestra _____.   2 Every tree _____.
3 Each new pupil _____.   4 Baked beans _____.

> **TIP**
> Remember, the **predicate** is all of the sentence except the subject.

B Add a **subject** to each of these predicates to make a sentence.

1 _____ sparkles with jewels.
2 _____ was very long.
3 _____ were under the table.
4 _____ gallop around the racecourse.

> **TIP**
> The **subject** of a sentence is the person or thing written about.

Adverbs tell us how, when or where something happens. Look at the picture.

TIP

A **phrase** is a group of words that does not have a main verb.

How did the rocket take off?

We could use a **single adverb**: The rocket took off **quickly**.

We could use an **adverb phrase** to make it more interesting.

The rocket took off **in a huge burst of flame**.

When did the rocket take off?

We could use a single adverb: The rocket took off **yesterday**.

We could use an adverb phrase to make it more interesting.

The rocket took off **early in the morning**.

Where did the rocket take off?

We could use a single adverb: The rocket took off **here**.

We could use an adverb phrase to make it more interesting.

The rocket took off **in the middle of the desert**.

Focus

A Say if the **adverb phrase** is telling you how, when or where.

1 over the fence   2 later that day   3 with great care

4 in the stormy sea 5 quickly and quietly 6 a week ago

B Copy the sentences. Underline the **adverb phrase** in each one.

1 My uncle came into the house with loud, thudding steps.

2 Yesterday morning, I planted some seeds.

3 The eagle built its nest on the mountain top.

Practice

A Use these **adverb phrases** in sentences of your own.

1 in the middle of the night
2 before sunrise
3 at the crossroads
4 from time to time
5 carefully and slowly
6 with great confidence

B Write a sentence with an adverb phrase to describe how, when or where each of these verbs happened.

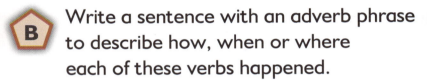

> **TIP**
> You can use any **verb tense**. You do not have to use **the verb family name**.

1 to mix
2 to measure
3 to leave
4 to discuss
5 to laugh
6 to cough

Extension

A Three of the following are **adverb phrases** and three are sentences. Copy the adverb phrases and add a **main verb** and any other words you need to make them into sentences.

1 before the first lesson
2 we'll meet at the corner
3 in front of the camera
4 gasping for breath
5 you must find that letter
6 simon rang the bell over and over again

B Find the three sentences from **A**. Write them with the correct punctuation.

Direct speech is when we write the actual words that someone said.

Inverted commas (speech marks) go before and after the spoken words.

Punctuation at the end of the spoken words comes <u>before</u> the inverted commas.

When a different person speaks, we begin a new line.

"The driver got the bus stuck under the bridge today," said Meg.
"What happened?" asked Mum.
"The police came and sent for a tow truck. It took them ages to get it free," explained Meg.
"Were you late for school?" asked Mum.
"Yes, we were!" said Meg.

Indirect speech is when we write about what a person said.
We <u>don't</u> use the actual spoken words.
We <u>don't</u> need inverted commas.

> **TIP**
> Indirect speech is sometimes called **reported speech**.

Meg told her mum that the bus had got stuck under the bridge. Mum wanted to know what happened and Meg said that the police came with a tow truck to free the bus. Mum asked Meg if she was late for school and Meg said that she was.

Focus

Say which of these sentences uses **direct speech** and which uses **indirect speech**.

1 "Look at my swimming certificate," said Len.

2 Sam said that he couldn't find the newspaper.

3 "Could you tell me the time?" asked Mo.

Practice

A Write each of these sentences using **indirect speech**.

1 "Would all passengers go to platform 8," said the voice over the loudspeaker.

2 "I like toast for breakfast," said Dad.

3 "Will you take my books back to the library?" asked Mum.

4 The teacher said, "Open your book at page 10."

5 "I'm really hungry!" said Sam.

B Write each of these sentences using **direct speech**.

1 Chris said that his book was very interesting.

2 Kim wanted to know how far they had to walk.

3 The farmer asked how many sheep had wandered off.

4 I asked Ben to turn on the radio.

5 Ali wanted to know the name of the river.

Extension

A Sam and Harry talk about what they watched on television last night. Write their conversation in **direct speech**.

Remember to:
- put inverted commas at the beginning and end of the spoken words
- put the punctuation after the spoken words and before the inverted commas
- begin a new line when a new person speaks.

B Write the same conversation between Sam and Harry in **indirect speech**.

Remember:
- you do not need inverted commas because you are not writing the actual spoken words.

Check-up 1

Adjectives

A Copy the sentences. Underline the **adjective phrases**.

1 Antarctica is a cold and frozen land.
2 The bicycle with the punctured tyre is mine.
3 The angry, wounded tiger ran into the jungle.

B Use these adjective phrases in sentences of your own.

1 brightly coloured   2 dirty and smelly   3 in the old coat

Prefixes

Use a **prefix** to make the opposite of each word.

1 legal   2 wise   3 behave   4 active   5 visible

Verbs

Copy the sentences. Underline the **auxiliary verbs**.

1 I am drawing a flower and a tree.
2 The dolphin might jump out of the water.
3 We should plough the field tomorrow.

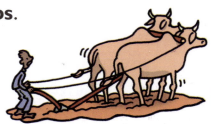

Pronouns

A Copy the sentences. Underline the **possessive pronouns**.

1 This towel is mine.   2 That baby of theirs is noisy.
3 This bicycle is hers.   4 Is this key yours?

B Use each of these possessive pronouns in sentences of your own.

1 his **2** ours **3** hers **4** theirs **5** mine **6** yours

Nouns

Write a **noun** that can be made from each verb.

1 to manage **2** to free **3** to paint **4** to laugh

Singular and plural

Complete each sentence by choosing the correct word.

1 The goats was / were on the road.
2 Every bird / birds had left the tree.
3 The choir have / has started singing.

Adverbs

Copy the sentences. Underline the **adverb phrases**.

1 The class listened in complete silence.
2 The parade will begin tomorrow at midday.
3 From the top of the hill I could see the town.

Sentences

A Write each of these sentences using **direct speech**.

1 David said that he had been on holiday.
2 Lynn wanted to know what time it was.

B Write each of these sentences in **indirect speech**.

1 "Where are we going?" asked Mike.
2 "It's too early to go to bed," moaned Maria.

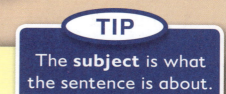

When the **subject** of a sentence does the action, the **verb** is called an **active verb**.

The **man bought** a ticket.

**subject of   what the
the sentence   subject did**

In this sentence 'bought' is the active verb.

When the subject of a sentence has the action done to it, the verb is called a **passive verb**.

The **ticket was bought** by the man.

**subject of   what was done
the sentence   to the subject**

In this sentence 'was bought' is the passive verb.

Focus

A Say which of these sentences is **active** and which is **passive**.

1 The stone broke the window.   The window was broken by the stone.

2 The work was marked by   The teacher marked the work.
the teacher.

3 The man cleaned the car.   The car was cleaned by the man.

B Find the **verb** in each sentence. Write whether the verb is active or passive.

1 The man banged on the desk.   **2** The ball was hit by the bat.

3 The bridge fell into the river.   **4** The volcano erupted today.

5 The library was broken into   **6** My dictionary was torn by
last night.   my baby brother.

A Rewrite each of these sentences. Change the verbs from **active** to **passive**. The first one is done for you.

1 Our teacher read a story.

A story was read by our teacher.

2 Dad painted the front door.

3 The cows ate the grass.

4 Some people heard thunder.

5 Sally collected the apples.

B Rewrite each of these sentences. Change the verbs from passive to active. The first one is done for you.

1 The mug was cracked by the boy.

The boy cracked the mug.

2 The windows were cleaned by the window cleaner.

3 The play was liked by the audience.

4 The house was shaded by trees.

5 The rabbits were caught by the farmer.

A Write sentences where each of these verbs is **active**, like this: The boy <u>carried</u> the logs.

1 to walk   **2** to lift   **3** to see

4 to write   **5** to cover   **6** to bury

B Rewrite the sentences from **A**, making the verbs **passive**.

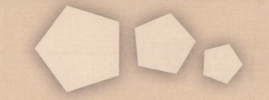

A **suffix** is a word ending.

The suffixes 'd' and 'ed' tell us that an action happened in the past.

She smile**d** at me. I smash**ed** the plate.

The suffix 'ing' with the verb 'to be' tells us that the action is in the **present tense** or the **past tense**.

I **am** throw**ing** the ball. I **was** throw**ing** the ball.

The suffix 'er' is used to make **comparative adjectives**, **comparative adverbs** and **nouns**.

Comparative adjectives	Comparative adverbs	Nouns
high/high**er**	slow/slow**er**	walk/walk**er**
soft/soft**er**	loud/loud**er**	sing/sing**er**

When we add 'ed', 'ing' or 'er' to words, we sometimes have to double the last letter. We usually double the last letter if the one before it is a single vowel.

skip	ski**pp**ing	ski**pp**ed	ski**pp**er
fit	fi**tt**ing	fi**tt**ed	fi**tt**er

Focus

TIP

Remember to double the last letter when needed.

A Add the **suffix** 'ed' to each of these.

1 warm   2 flip   3 wrap   4 clean   5 slip

B Add the **suffix** 'ing' to each of these.

1 run   2 walk   3 jump   4 hop   5 hit

C Add the **suffix** 'er' to each of these.

1 catch   2 tap   3 help   4 shop   5 count

Practice

Copy the sentences. Add the **suffix** 'ed', 'ing' or 'er' to complete each sentence.

1. This ice cream is big_____ than that one.
2. The pirates were look_____ for the treasure.
3. We search_____ and search_____ but we could not find it.
4. The fastest run_____ won the prize.
5. The audience clap_____ the singer.
6. Cook_____ is one of my hobbies.

Extension

A Use the **suffix** 'ing' and the verb 'to be' to change these sentences into the **present continuous tense**.

1. The birds circled overhead.
2. A new family moved into the village.
3. The garage door creaked in the wind.
4. I tried hard with all my sums.
5. They shopped for a new school uniform.

B Use the suffix 'ed' and miss out the verb 'to be' to change these sentences into the **simple past tense**.

1. We are wondering why the bus is late.
2. I am posting a letter to my friend.
3. They are picking a team captain.
4. He is sailing into the harbour.
5. You are planting the seeds.

A **simple sentence** has a **subject** and a **verb**.
A simple sentence is also called a **main clause**.
A **clause** is a group of words that makes sense and has a **finite verb**.
A finite verb forms a **tense** and has a **subject**.

The man knocked on the door.

subject   finite verb

A compound sentence is made up of two main clauses, usually joined by 'and', 'but' or 'or'.

The man **knocked** on the door **and rang** the bell.

finite verb   finite verb

1st main clause = The man knocked on the door.
2nd main clause = [He] rang the bell.

Focus

A Add a **finite verb** to each subject to make a **simple sentence**.

1 Our cat   2 The wind   3 This book
4 All the girls 5 The tall tree   6 My sister

B Copy the sentences. Underline the finite verbs.

1 My brother plays the piano.   2 I am looking for my shoes.
3 Lightning flashed all around.   4 The pond is full of weeds.
5 The boys cleaned the bicycle.   6 I need a new pen.

Practice

TIP

Use 'and', 'but' or 'or' to join the sentences.

Make **compound sentences** from these pairs of simple sentences.

1 The band came down the street.
It went into the park.

2 We played very well.
We didn't win the match.

3 The sky grew dark.
The rain began falling.

4 The volcano erupted.
Lava poured down its sides.

5 I might have an apple.
I might have an orange.

Extension

A Add another **main clause** to these **simple sentences** to make **compound sentences**.

1 The apple was rotten and _____

2 I could see the town in the distance but _____

3 My brother and I quarrelled but _____

4 He wanted to read my book or _____

5 The lion roared and _____

6 _____ and we enjoyed ourselves.

7 _____ but I couldn't sleep.

8 _____ or we can stay indoors.

9 _____ and he dug the garden.

10 _____ but she didn't win.

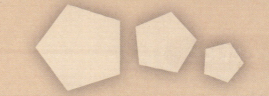

Adjectives are sometimes called describing words because they tell us more about **nouns**.

an **unhappy** farmer

a **neat** hedge

Possessive adjectives tell us who possesses (owns) a noun.

This is **his** badge.

This is **her** horse.

TIP
Possessive adjectives describe a noun, for example: my book.

These are possessive adjectives: my, your, his, her, our, its, their
A **possessive pronoun** stands in place of a possessive adjective and a noun, for example: This book is mine.

Focus

A Say these using **possessive adjectives**.

1 This book is mine.

2 That toy is his.

3 The cat is hers.

4 This garden is ours.

5 The school bags are theirs.

6 These books are yours.

B Copy the sentences. Underline the possessive adjectives.

1 The computer in our classroom is not working.
2 Your memory must be very good.
3 The castle was very old and its tower was in ruins.
4 Joe helped his friend to find the football.

Practice

Copy the sentences. Fill each gap with a suitable **possessive adjective**.

1 I'll let you have _____ new address when we move.
2 The twins found it easy to do _____ homework.
3 Katy was pleased because _____ friend was coming to stay.
4 The cat rolled in the dust and _____ coat got dirty.

Extension

A Write an ordinary **adjective** and a **possessive adjective** to describe these nouns, like this:
His colourful picture.

1 camera   2 cough   3 breakfast
4 table   5 birthday   6 jacket

It is easy to mix up 'its' and 'it's'.
'Its' means 'belonging to'.   A zebra looks like a horse but **its** coat is striped.
'It's' means 'it is'.   **It's** very warm today.

B Copy and complete the sentences with 'its' or 'it's'.

1 "_____ a goal!" screamed Jenny.
2 _____ windier today than it was yesterday.
3 The kitten put out _____ sharp claws.

To make sentences more interesting we can use **adjective phrases** and **adjective clauses**.
They tell us more about a **noun** or **pronoun** in the **main clause**.
Adjective phrases have no **finite** verb.

The boy **with the twin sister** was not at school.
The flowers, **bright and colourful**, grew under the window.

Adjective clauses begin with 'who', 'which' or 'that' and have a finite verb.
We use 'who' when we are writing about a person.

The nurse took care of the man **who** had broken his arm.

We use 'which' or 'that' when we are writing about an animal or thing.

The key, **which** fits this lock, is lost.
I saw the birds **that** are nesting in the garage.

Focus

A Say if these are **adjective phrases** or **adjective clauses**.

1 with great care 　　　　　 2 which is on the table

3 who wears a red hat 　　　 4 cold and unhappy

5 three red and orange 　　 6 that comes into the garden

B Copy the sentences. Underline the adjective clause.
Put a ring around the **noun** or **pronoun** it tells us about.

1 I delivered the package that my mother had given to me.

2 Mark wrote to his friend who lives in Australia.

3 The badge, which I bought at the zoo, shows a zebra.

4 I want to find the boy who owns this bicycle.

5 Can you lend me the book that you've just finished reading?

Copy the sentences. Use 'who' or 'which' to fill each gap.

1 The journey, _____ they made on foot, took a long time.
2 Will you find someone _____ can take care of the hamster?
3 I have taken the chair, _____ had a broken arm, to be mended.
4 There were three passengers _____ had lost their tickets.
5 Give the pencil, _____ has an eraser on the end, to Al.

Extension

A Add **adjective clauses** to these **main clauses** to complete each sentence.

1 I baked the bread _____.
2 They looked for the girl _____.
3 We visited the old woman _____.
4 I went to the house _____.
5 We saw the boy _____.

B Add main clauses to these adjective clauses to complete each sentence.

1 _____ who likes to play football.
2 _____ which grows in our garden.
3 _____ that I like best.
4 _____ which fell on our house.
5 _____ that was left in the bowl.

TIP
The **adjective clause** needs a **finite verb**.

TIP
The **main clause** needs a **finite verb**.

TIP
Auxiliary verbs are helper verbs.

Sometimes we need more than one **verb** to make a sentence work properly. We need to use an **auxiliary verb**. The verb families 'to be' and 'to have' are often used as auxiliary verbs.

My dad **is working** in the garden.
The candle **has burnt** very low.

The words 'can' and 'may' are used as auxiliary verbs.

can = able to   He **can** answer that question.
may = has permission to   You **may** leave the room.

'Shall' and 'will' are also used as auxiliary verbs. They form the future tense.

shall = use after 'I' and 'we'   I **shall** go out.
will = use after 'you', 'they', 'he', 'she' and 'it'   They **will** go out.

Focus

A Say what the **auxiliary verb** in each sentence is.

1 I have looked for the book.   **2** She can climb over the fence.

3 We shall miss the bus.   **4** You may have an ice cream.

5 Arun is walking home.   **6** The tiger was hunting.

B Copy the sentences. Underline the auxiliary verbs.

1 The picture was hanging on that wall.

2 I have forgotten to do my homework.

3 I can swim the length of the pool.

4 We may buy some sweets.

A Copy the sentences.
Use 'may' or 'can' to fill each gap.

1 This book is quite difficult but I am sure you _____ read it.

2 You _____ go out to play when you have changed your clothes.

3 You _____ get to the top of that tree with a ladder.

4 You _____ not cross the road by yourself.

B Copy the sentences.
Use 'shall' or 'will' to fill each gap.

1 I _____ write very neatly in my new book.

2 "You _____ need new shoes soon," said Mum.

3 She _____ find these sums very difficult.

4 We _____ have to finish this later.

5 _____ you be home by five o'clock?

Extension

Write sentences of your own using these pairs of verbs.
Underline the **auxiliary verb** in each sentence.

1 has received   **2** will recognise

3 can finish   **4** may drop

5 is climbing   **6** was carrying

7 shall obey   **8** will do

9 may begin   **10** can find

TIP

Adverb phrases and **adverb clauses** do the same job as **adverbs**. They give us more information about **verbs**.

To make sentences more interesting, we can use **adverb phrases** and **adverb clauses**. Adverb phrases have no **finite verb**.

The postman calls **early each morning**.
The mouse ran across the floor **quickly and quietly**.

Adverb clauses begin with **conjunctions** and have a finite verb.

The train stopped **because** the engine **broke** down.

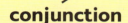

conjunction   **finite verb**

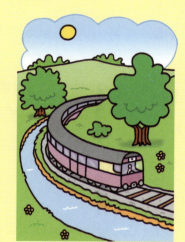

The adverb clause 'because the engine broke down' tells us why the train had stopped.

The train will start again **when** they **fix** the engine.

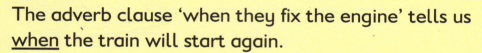

conjunction   **finite verb**

The adverb clause 'when they fix the engine' tells us <u>when</u> the train will start again.

Adverb clauses can also begin with other conjunctions, such as 'even though' and 'even if'.

Focus

A   Say if these are **adverb phrases** or **adverb clauses**.

1 late last night

2 because it is raining

3 unless you wash your hands

4 on the edge of the road

5 in a great hurry

6 when I have finished eating

7 over the cliff

8 entered the dark cave

B Copy the sentences. Underline the adverb clause.
Put a ring around the **verb** it tells us about.

1 The prisoner escaped because the guard was asleep.

2 I can't polish my shoes because there is no polish.

3 We shall have to walk unless we catch the bus.

Practice

A Copy the sentences. Choose words from the box to complete the
adverb clauses.

> because   unless   although   even if   if   even though

1 We shall go to the village shop ----------------- we have time.

2 You cannot ride your bike ----------------- you wear your helmet.

3 I have to find my bag ----------------- I am late for school.

Extension

Adverb clauses can come at the beginning of a sentence. An adverb
clause at the beginning of a sentence is followed by a comma.
When they fix the engine, the train will start again.

A Add adverb clauses to these **main clauses** to complete the
sentences.

1 The garage was broken into ----------------- .

2 ----------------- , you will get wet.

3 You must obey the rules ----------------- .

B Add main clauses to the adverb clauses to complete the sentences.

1 ----------------- because the scissors are blunt.

2 Although I am disappointed, ----------------- .

Adjectives

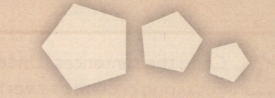

Some **adjectives** are formed from **verbs**.

Verb	Adjective	Example
to bend	bent	a **bent** pin
to burn	burnt	the **burnt** toast
to shine	shiny	the **shiny** coin

Some verbs are used as adjectives.

Verb	Use as adjective
to rock	**rocking** chair
to skate	**skating** rink
to build	**building** block

Some adjectives are formed from **nouns**.

Noun	Adjective	Example
skill	skilful	a **skilful** player
child	childish	a **childish** joke
danger	dangerous	a **dangerous** road

Some nouns are used as adjectives.

Noun	Use as adjective
book	**book** cover
window	**window**sill
town	**town** hall

Focus

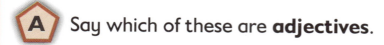

A Say which of these are **adjectives**.

1 happiness   2 to cry   3 fool   4 to paint

5 friend   6 to run   7 dirty   8 great

B Copy the sentences. Underline the adjective.
Write whether it is formed from a **noun** or a **verb**.

1 The crying baby was in the pram.

2 The wooden hut was never used.

3 The dried flowers were thrown away.

4 The golden necklace was kept locked away.

Practice

A Use the **verbs** in the box to make **adjectives** to complete these sentences.

1 I practised diving into the _____ pool.

2 The _____ storm woke me up.

3 I have finished my _____ book.

4 I can't hold a fork with my _____ arm.

to read
to swim
to terrify
to break

B Use the **nouns** in the box to make adjectives to complete the sentences.

1 The _____ path hurt my feet.

2 The box is a _____ shape.

3 Thank you for your _____ donation.

4 The _____ boy needed a wash.

rectangle
stone
generosity
dirt

Extension

Use the following **nouns** as **adjectives** in sentences of your own.

1 village   2 fire   3 cricket

4 water   5 tennis   6 paper

Check-up 2

Sentences

A Copy the sentences. Underline the **main clause** in each one.

1 I have to water the plants, although it rained today.
2 Before the sun sets, we must find our way home.

B Join each pair of sentences using 'who' or 'that'.
You may have to miss out some words when you join the sentences.

1 I needed a new bag. I could take it to school.
2 We have two mice. They are white.

Adverbs

Add an **adverb clause** to each of these main clauses.

1 The ring slipped off my finger _____.
2 The woman typed the letter _____.
3 _____, we found an old house.

Suffixes

A Add the suffix 'ed', 'ing' or 'er' to complete these sentences.

1 The clean_____ swept and polish_____ the floor.
2 The teach_____ was look_____ for some chalk.

B Add 'ing' to these words.

1 hit   2 skip   3 run   4 chat   5 sip   6 bat

Verbs

A Underline the **verb** in each sentence.
Write whether the verb is **active** or **passive**.

1 The explosion was heard for miles around.

2 The buses crawled slowly along the road.

3 The letter was delivered by the postman.

B Write these active sentences as passive sentences.

1 The man built the fence.

2 The cat chased the mouse.

3 The farmer planted the seeds.

C Write these passive sentences as active sentences.

1 The car was cleaned by the young boy.

2 My work was marked by the teacher.

3 The tree was blown down by the wind.

D Fill the gap with 'can' or 'may' to complete each sentence.

1 The children _____ have a pet if they look after it.

2 I _____ meet you at one o'clock.

3 You _____ write more neatly than that.

Adjectives

A Write the **adjectives** that are formed from these nouns and verbs.

1 to fall   **2** fright   **3** to fry   **4** rock

B Use these **possessive adjectives** in sentences of your own.

1 my   **2** her   **3** its   **4** your

TIP

Adding a **suffix** often changes the spelling. Always check in a dictionary.

A **suffix** is a word ending.

A suffix added to a **verb family name** changes the tense.

Verb family name	Suffix 'd' or 'ed'	Suffix 'ing'
to talk	talk**ed**	talk**ing**
to smile	smile**d**	smil**ing**
to clean	clean**ed**	clean**ing**

Adding a suffix can also change the job that the word does in a sentence.

Word		Change by adding suffix	
use	= verb	use**ful**	= adjective
pain	= noun	pain**ful**	= adjective
operate	= verb	opera**tion**	= noun
imagine	= verb	imagina**tion**	= noun
happy	= adjective	happ**iness**	= abstract noun
weak	= adjective	weak**ness**	= abstract noun

Here are some more common suffixes.

amuse – amuse**ment**	manage – manage**able**
tire – tire**less**	serve – serv**ant**

Focus

A   Say what the **noun** made from each **verb family name** is.

1   to laugh   **2**   to invite   **3**   to sing

4   to manage   **5**   to build   **6**   to explain

B Copy the sentences. Use words with the suffix 'ful', 'tion' or 'ness' to complete them. The words in brackets are clues.

1 (Dark) falls quickly near the equator.

2 You need to be very (care) if you climb these rocks.

3 He is very keen on sport and (fit).

4 The view from the top of the mountain was (wonder).

Practice

A Add **suffixes** to these words to change them into **adjectives**.

1 beauty 2 care 3 hope 4 believe 5 enjoy

B Use three of the adjectives you have made in sentences of your own.

C Add suffixes to these words to change them into **abstract nouns**.

1 weak 2 situate 3 gentle 4 satisfy 5 kind

D Use three of the abstract nouns you have made in sentences of your own.

Extension

A Here are some words with useful **suffixes.** Use each of the words in the box in sentences of your own.

famous decision entrance
curious different

B Write a word with a suffix to match each of these definitions.

1 willing to help   help _ _ _
2 someone's job   occupa _ _ _ _ _
3 the opposite of daylight   dark _ _ _ _ _
4 very good at something   skil _ _ _ _
5 very unhappy   miser _ _ _ _ _
6 doing as you are told   obedi _ _ _ _

TIP

Use a dictionary to help you.

All **sentences** begin with a capital letter.
All sentences end with either:

- a **full stop** — The music was very loud.
- a **question mark** — What time is it?
- an **exclamation mark** — The house is burning!

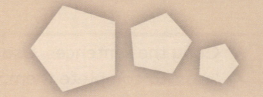

Commas are used to help us understand the sense of a sentence. We use commas between items in a list.

I had to learn to spell anteater, elephant, kangaroo, panda and zebra.

We use commas to separate spoken words from the rest of the sentence.

"I came early to get a good seat," said Ben.

We use commas after 'yes' and 'no' and before question tags.

Yes, I do like ice cream.   No, I will not be late.

This is a good photograph, isn't it?   You'll bring milk, won't you?

TIP

We use 'and' or 'or' between the last two items in a list instead of a **comma**.

Focus

A   Where do the missing **commas** go?

1   "I have found your book" said Mum.

2   No that isn't right.

3   You like apples don't you?

4   Yes I will be there on time.

B   Copy the sentences. Add commas where they are needed.

1   I did maths English PE and music in school today.

2   Peter lost his pen his ruler his eraser and his pencil sharpener.

Practice

A The punctuation has been missed out after the spoken words. Copy each sentence and add a **comma**, a **question mark** or an **exclamation mark**.

1 "The shop is closed" said Tom.

2 "I'm going to be really late" cried Jay.

3 "Is it raining" asked Nina.

B Add commas to these sentences.

1 Yes I would like to go to the cinema.

2 He hurt his arm falling off his bike didn't he?

3 You will find the key won't you?

Extension

Commas often go around **phrases** and **clauses** in sentences.
The phrases and clauses give us extra information.
If they were left out, the sentence would still make sense.

The clown, **running around the ring,** made everyone laugh.
The clown made everyone laugh.

Copy the sentences.
Put commas around the phrases and clauses in these sentences.

1 The customer angry and impatient shouted at the shop assistant.

2 My sister who is four years younger than me starts school next week.

3 The old tree which had been dead for years was cut down.

4 The house freshly painted was up for sale.

5 The village which is on the other side of the river is where my aunt lives.

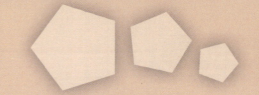

A **pronoun** takes the place of a noun.

The driver parked the van outside the shop.
He parked the van outside the shop.

These pronouns are called **relative pronouns**: 'who', 'which' and 'that'.

Relative pronouns are special because they do two jobs.

- They take the place of nouns.
- They act as **conjunctions** and they are related to the noun that comes before them in the sentence.

The passenger caught the train.
The passenger caught the train **that** was going to London.

'Who' is always used for people.
'Which' and 'that' are used for animals and things.

Focus

A Which would you say?

1 The door who opened.   or   The door that opened.

2 The doctor who helped.   or   The doctor that helped.

3 The tiger who roared.   or   The tiger that roared.

B Copy the sentence. Fill the gaps with 'who' or 'which'.

1 The cat, _____ comes into our garden, is black.

2 The park, _____ has a boating lake, is nearby.

3 Jack is the boy _____ has just come to our school.

4 The key, _____ opens that cupboard, is in my desk.

TIP

You will need to miss out some words when you join the sentences.

Practice

Join each pair of sentences using 'who' or 'that'.

1 I found an old coin. The coin was used in Roman times.

2 We have two cousins. Our cousins live by the sea.

3 Sam bought a book. The book was about fishing.

Extension

The **relative pronouns** 'whom' and 'whose' are used in a special way. 'Whom' is used for people as the **object** of a verb.

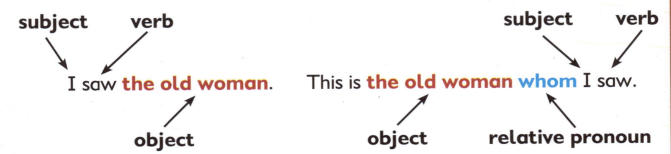

subject   **verb**   **subject**   **verb**

    I saw **the old woman**.   This is **the old woman whom** I saw.

        object   **object**   **relative pronoun**

'Whose' is used to replace a **possessive adjective**.

    possessive adjective

This is the woman. **Her** cat is called Tom.
This is the woman **whose** cat is called Tom.

        relative pronoun

Copy the sentences. Use 'whom' or 'whose' to fill the gaps.

1 I know the man _____ car was stolen.

2 From _____ did you borrow this book?

3 _____ bag is this?

4 This is my cousin _____ I am going to stay with.

5 Sam has a pet snake _____ name is Wriggles.

Sentences contain **clauses**.
A **main clause** is a sentence in itself.
The man won the race.

It has a **subject**: the man
It has a **predicate**: won the race
It has a **finite verb**: won

An **adjective clause** tells us more about the
noun in the main clause, and has a **finite verb**.
I **want** to see the man who **won** the race.

main clause:	I want to see the man
adjective clause:	who won the race

> **TIP**
> **Adjective clauses** begin with 'who', 'which' or 'that'.

finite verb = want
finite verb = won

An **adverb clause** tells us more about the **verb**
in the main clause, and also has a finite verb.

The man **won** the race because he **ran**
so quickly.

main clause:	The man won the race
adverb clause:	because he ran so quickly

> **TIP**
> **Adverb clauses** begin with a conjunction.

finite verb = won
finite verb = ran

Focus

A Say if these are **adjective clauses** or **adverb clauses**.

1 … who wore a yellow scarf.   **2** … after I have finished my jobs.

3 … before the sun went down.   **4** … that has been cut down.

B Copy the sentences. Underline the **main clauses**.

1 The animal slipped into the pool before the sun came up.

2 After the match, the winners were presented with the cup.

3 I will practise my handwriting because I want it to be neat.

Copy the sentences. Underline the **adjective clauses** and put a ring around the **adverb clauses**.

1 Although it is warm today, you must take your coat.

2 I will wash the bicycle that is muddy.

3 The trip was cancelled because rain was pouring down.

4 We will invite the twins who live on the farm.

5 The head teacher, who was very tall, gave out the sports prizes.

Extension

> **TIP**
> **Adjective clauses** begin with 'who', 'which' or 'that'.

 A Complete these sentences by adding **adjective clauses**.

1 This is the kitten _____

2 Have you seen the film _____

3 We saw the rider _____

4 Can I speak to the teacher _____

5 They met their friend _____

 B Complete these sentences by adding **adverb clauses**. You can choose a conjunction from the box to begin your adverb clause.

> because   before   when
> after   although

1 The little boy was naughty _____

2 I will eat all my vegetables _____

3 The zebra walked to the waterhole _____

4 _____ you can watch that television programme.

5 I must write a shopping list _____

Unit 21 Verbs

When we use **verbs** for something that has happened in the past, we use **past tenses**.

Simple past tense
We add 'ed' or 'd' to most verb family names to make the **simple past tense**.

The lion hunt**ed**.   The nurse smile**d**.

Some verbs do not follow these rules.

to write – wrote	to go – went	to buy – bought

Past continuous tense
When an action has gone on for some time, or something else happens at the same time, we use the **past continuous tense**.

We make this with the simple past tense of the verb 'to be' + 'ing'.

The lion **was** hunt**ing** all night.
The nurse **was** smil**ing** as she bandaged my arm.

Past perfect tense
If two things have happened in the past but one is further back in time, we use the **past perfect tense**.
We make this using 'had' + the simple past tense.

The lion **had** hunt**ed** all night and then went to sleep.
The nurse **had** bandag**ed** my arm and then spoken to my mother.

Focus

A   Say the **simple past tense** of these **verb family names**.

1   to see   **2**   to think   **3**   to ride   **4**   to sleep

5   to run   **6**   to fly   **7**   to speak   **8**   to come

B Copy the sentences. Underline the **past tense verbs**.

1 They had lived in the town before they moved to the country.
2 We were watching the film when my friend arrived.
3 Dad had come home from work early so he took us to the park.

Practice

Copy and complete this table, using the three ways you know of making the **past tense**.

Verb family name	Simple past	Past continuous	Past perfect
to talk	I talked	I was talking	I had talked
to find	we _____	we _____	we _____
to see	they _____	they _____	they _____
to bring	you _____	you _____	you _____
to throw	we _____	we _____	we _____
to catch	she _____	she _____	she _____
to cry	he _____	he _____	she _____

Extension

Write a sentence using **past tenses** that include each pair of actions.
Action 1 happens first, before Action 2. The first one is done for you.

1 Action 1: watch a film   Action 2: go to bed
   I had watched a film before I went to bed.
2 Action 1: do homework   Action 2: play tennis
3 Action 1: eat breakfast   Action 2: post arrives
4 Action 1: write a story   Action 2: go home

Direct speech is when we write the actual words that are spoken.

"I need to move these boxes and put them over there," said Paul.

Paul said, "I need to move these boxes and put them over there."

Sometimes we split the spoken words so we have to be very careful with the punctuation.

"I need to move these boxes," said Paul, "and put them over there."

The sentence has been split by the words 'said Paul', so we use two sets of inverted commas and put a comma after 'said Paul'.

"I need to move these boxes," said Paul. "I need to put them over there."

This time Paul has said two sentences. We still use two sets of inverted commas but we put a full stop after 'said Paul' before we begin the next sentence.

Focus

A What words would you use instead of 'said' if you were:

1 asking a question? **2** speaking quietly?

3 speaking loudly? **4** very upset?

5 frightened? **6** really happy?

B Copy the sentences. Underline the spoken words.

1 "I won this medal," said Sara, "for coming first in the race."

2 "Where did you find that old coin?" asked the teacher.

3 "You can ring me at work," explained Nick, "if you need to get in touch with me."

4 The climber shouted, "Get away from the edge!"

5 "I'm not very musical," mumbled David. "I like sport better."

Copy the sentences. Put in the missing **punctuation** and **capital letters**.

1 that was a good goal shouted Sandy but we have to score another one

2 go to the shop and buy some bread said Mum the money is in my purse

3 this photograph was taken last year explained Kim we were visiting my grandmother

4 we must be very quiet whispered the girl or we'll wake the baby

5 i'm very tired moaned Chris I stayed up too late last night

6 can you find your school shoes asked Dad and give them a polish

Extension

The words in the box can all be used instead of 'said'.

cried
yelled
muttered
laughed
sobbed
shrieked
boasted

Use a dictionary so you understand what each word means.
Use each word in **direct speech** sentences of your own.
Try to use some of them between the spoken words.

> **TIP**
> A clause has a **finite verb**.

A **simple sentence** is made up of one main clause.
The hawk **soared** in the air.

A **compound sentence** is made up of two or
more simple sentences joined by 'and', 'but' or 'or'.

simple sentence:	The hawk soared in the air.
simple sentence:	We watched it for some time.
compound sentence:	The hawk soared in the air **and** we watched it for some time.
simple sentence:	We were caught in a traffic jam.
simple sentence:	We made it on time.
compound sentence:	We were caught in a traffic jam **but** we made it on time.
simple sentence:	It might rain tomorrow.
simple sentence:	It might be fine.
compound sentence:	It might rain tomorrow **or** it might be fine.

Focus

A Say if these are **phrases** or **clauses**.

1 after it rained   **2** yellow and orange   **3** the dirty water

4 when we arrived   **5** during the night   **6** because it is broken

B Make **compound sentences** from these pairs of simple sentences.

1 My sandal is broken. I think I can mend it.

2 The library was busy. There was nowhere to sit.

3 I might have pizza for lunch. I might have soup.

4 The bird's feathers were blue. Its beak was yellow.

Practice

Copy the **compound sentences**.
Underline the two **main clauses** in each sentence and put a ring around the **conjunction**.

1 The famous explorer went to Africa and she stayed there for many years.

2 The volcano erupted and lava poured down its sides.

3 I enjoy playing basketball but I am too tired to play now.

4 Are you going shopping on Friday or will you wait until Saturday morning?

5 It's my birthday today and I'm going to have a party.

Extension

TIP

Use these **conjunctions** in the sentences: 'and', 'but' or 'or'.

Add a **conjunction** and a **main clause** to make each of these **simple sentences** into **compound sentences**.

1 The diver was looking for pearls _____.

2 My head is aching _____.

3 The factory is closing down _____.

4 I might go for a swim _____.

5 It might rain today _____.

6 Becky watched the hockey match _____.

Sentences

A **simple sentence** is made up of one main clause.

The election was held on Thursday.

A **compound sentence** is made up of two or more simple sentences joined by 'and', 'but' or 'or'.

The election was held on Thursday **and** the result was announced on Friday.

> **TIP**
> The clauses that are less important are called **subordinate clauses**.

A **complex sentence** is made up of two or more clauses that are not of equal importance.
There is one **main clause** in a complex sentence. Other clauses are joined to it by these words.

Conjunctions				Pronouns
before	where	unless	so	who
until	because	when	if	which
although	while	after	as	whose
wherever	even though			

The house had been empty for years before we bought it.

main clause   **subordinate clause**

The clause 'before we bought it' is not a sentence on its own. It needs a main clause to make sense.

Focus

A   Say if these are **main clauses** or **subordinate clauses**.

1   it's cold today   2   the wind is blowing   3   even though I like it

4   when I get back   5   as the door opened   6   which is very long

B Copy these **complex sentences**. Underline the main clause in each sentence.

1 The guitar was broken before I borrowed it.

2 We climbed the mountain although it was very steep.

3 My sister will come over when she has finished work.

4 The Lees have a son called Mark who loves to play the piano.

Practice

TIP

Don't use 'and', 'but' or 'or'.

Join these pairs of **simple sentences** to make **complex sentences**.

1 The microscope isn't working. I checked it this morning.

2 We are going on holiday. We have bought two new suitcases.

3 The flowers died. I watered them every day.

4 We saw the wrecked ship. It had crashed on the rocks.

Extension

A Complete these as **compound sentences**.

1 The sheep were grazing in the field _____.

2 She put plates on the table _____.

3 I saw a shooting star _____.

4 I left my bag on the bus _____.

B Complete these as **complex sentences**.

1 He was very frightened _____.

2 The children had to play inside _____.

3 I enjoyed the adventure story _____.

4 We were almost asleep _____.

We need to look very carefully at what we write to see if we can improve it.

We can improve our writing by choosing better words.

I **got** a **nice** present for my birthday.

'Got' and 'nice' are words that are often used, but there are better words.

I **received** a **wonderful** present for my birthday.

We can improve our writing by expanding it.

Adding words, phrases and clauses make it more interesting.

The elephant **drank** the water.

The **large, grey** elephant **stretched out its long trunk to take a drink of refreshing water from the cool, shady pool.**

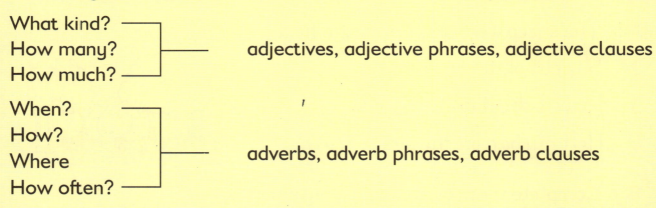

Look at each sentence you write and ask yourself whether you could add more details to answer these questions.

What kind?
How many?   adjectives, adjective phrases, adjective clauses
How much?

When?
How?
Where   adverbs, adverb phrases, adverb clauses
How often?

Focus

A Think of better words for:

1 got   **2** nice   **3** pretty   **4** said   **5** cold   **6** hot

B Rewrite these sentences to improve them.
Replace the underlined words with more interesting words.

1 Our <u>nice</u> hedge has grown <u>quite a bit</u> this spring.

2 "I've <u>got a lot of</u> work to do," <u>said</u> Harry.

3 I <u>like</u> <u>cold</u> weather because I've <u>got</u> a really warm coat.

4 "I <u>like</u> this book <u>a lot</u>," <u>said</u> John.

Practice

Improve these sentences to give details that answer the questions in the brackets.

1 The trees are growing.   (What kind? Where?)

2 The children played football.   (What kind? Where? How?)

3 The jockey won the race.   (What kind? When? How?)

4 Can you see the butterfly?   (What kind? Where?)

5 I walked into the town.   (How? What kind? When?)

Extension

Improve these sentences by including:
• more interesting words than 'got', 'said', 'like', 'bit', 'nice', 'lot', 'big' and 'little'
• words, phrases and clauses that give the reader more detail.

1 A little bird sat on a tree.   2 The bus got stuck.

3 "I've lost my ticket," said Lin.   4 Would you like a lolly?

5 The wind was a bit strong.   6 I got a nice jacket.

7 You can get a lot in this bucket.   8 That meal was nice.

9 "Did you see the big bull?" said Mehdi.

A **paragraph** is a group of sentences about one main idea. Dividing a long piece of writing into paragraphs makes it easier for the reader to follow. The beginning of a piece of writing starts at the **margin**. The paragraphs in the piece of writing are **indented** (moved away from the margin).

<u>Morning on the Farm</u>

Early morning on the farm was always a busy time. Cows had to be milked. Chickens had to be fed and many other jobs had to be done.

Anna climbed out of bed as soon as her alarm went off. She washed and dressed quickly as she had many things to do before breakfast.

When she arrived in the kitchen, her mother was already busy. She was baking bread and getting things ready for the first meal of the day. Anna set the table and then went outside.

After an hour of hard work, Anna had only the chickens to feed before she could have breakfast. She scattered the corn about the yard, washed her hands under the outside tap and went inside.

Each paragraph is about one main idea.

Paragraph 1: Introducing the reader to the farm.
Paragraph 2: Anna gets up.
Paragraph 3: Anna goes to the kitchen.
Paragraph 4: Anna does jobs on the farm.

Focus

Write the first three **paragraphs** of a story called 'The Dark Cave'. Use this as your paragraph plan.

Paragraph 1: Give a detailed description of the cave.
Paragraph 2: Introduce two characters who are exploring the cave.
Paragraph 3: Explain what happens to the two characters in the cave.

Remember that you are not writing the whole story so you do not have to finish everything in the third paragraph.

Read these **paragraphs** about animal environments and answer the questions.

Animals live in many different environments such as hot, dry deserts, freezing polar regions and in high mountains.

In the desert, temperatures can reach over 50°C during the day. There is not much water and animals have to keep cool by sheltering underground or in shady areas. Animals that do spend time in the sun move in a special way so that as little of their bodies as possible touches the hot sand.

In the polar regions, the temperature can fall lower than −80°C in the winter. Here, animals have to keep warm and one way to do this is to make dens under the snow.

Living in the mountains, animals often experience low temperatures and harsh winds. They survive by sheltering in caves or on rock ledges at night. They come out during the day to find food.

1 How many paragraphs has the writer used?

2 For each paragraph, write a sentence to explain the main idea.

Extension

A Find a short story that you have enjoyed reading. Answer these questions about the first four **paragraphs**.

1 What is the main idea in each paragraph?

2 Explain why the first paragraph is, or is not, a good opening to the story.

B Choose one of the following titles and write one paragraph of five to ten sentences about it. Underline one sentence in your paragraph to show the main idea.

- A Really Bad Day!
- Looking After a Pet
- My Favourite Sport

Check-up 3

Adjectives

A Copy these sentences and underline the **adjective phrase** in each.

1 Eight large, hissing geese crossed the road.
2 The sea, calm and blue, sparkled in the sunlight.
3 The elephant with the longest tusks is the oldest.

B Copy the sentences. Fill each gap with a suitable **possessive adjective**.

1 .... boots were dirty so we had to clean them.
2 Sam and .... friend went camping.
3 They packed .... bags before breakfast.

C Add an **adjective clause** to complete each sentence.

1 This is the rocket ....
2 We saw the shopkeeper ....
3 I went to the old house ....

D Make **adjectives** from these **nouns** and **verbs**.

1 to colour   2 grass   3 to frighten   4 to scream
5 bravery   6 envy   7 wood   8 to burn

Prefixes

Add a **prefix** to each word to make its opposite.

1 like   2 capable   3 honest   4 tidy   5 legal

Verbs

A Copy the sentences.
Underline the **auxiliary verb** in each sentence.

1 We must find our key.

2 If you go early, you might get a good seat.

3 I am looking for a new book to read.

B Copy these sentences.
Use the auxiliary verbs 'can' or 'may' to fill the gaps.

1 We _____ see the windmill from here.

2 You _____ have more potatoes when you have finished those.

3 If you _____ tidy the bookcase I will be very pleased.

C Copy the sentences.
Choose the **singular** or **plural** verb to complete each one.

1 The penguins was/were diving for fish.

2 The herd of cows need/needs to be milked.

3 Six dollars is/are the price of the tickets.

D Rewrite these sentences, changing the verb from **passive** to **active**.

1 The cake was eaten by the children.

2 The topmost leaves were eaten by the giraffes.

3 The window was broken by a stone.

E Copy the sentences.
Underline the **past tense** verbs in each one.

1 Our newspaper was delivered late today.

2 The gardener had cut the hedge before the birds built their nests.

3 I finished the quiz in ten minutes.

Pronouns

A Use **possessive pronouns** to replace the underlined words.

1 May I ride your bicycle? <u>My bicycle</u> has a puncture.

2 Their car is newer than <u>our car</u>.

3 You know that pen you found? Sally says it's <u>her pen</u>.

B Join each pair of sentences using a **relative pronoun**.

1 Freddy watched a programme. It was about whales.

2 I have an uncle. He is a policeman.

3 Have you seen the kittens? They were born on the farm.

Nouns

Write a **noun** that is formed from each of these verbs.

1 to write 2 to imagine 3 to grow

4 to play 5 to injure 6 to live

Adverbs

A Copy the sentences.
Underline the **adverb phrases**.

1 Two days ago I visited my aunty.

2 The boy kicked the ball hard and straight.

3 The fox made its den in the middle of the wood.

B Write an **adverb clause** to complete each sentence.

1 The match was cancelled _____.

2 _____, you will feel better.

3 I will go swimming again _____.

Suffixes

A Change these verb family names into the **present continuous tense**, using the **suffix** 'ing'.

1 to write   I _____
2 to live   we _____
3 to stop   he _____
4 to receive they _____

B Change these verb family names into the **simple past tense** using the suffixes 'ed' or 'd'.

1 to paint   we _____
2 to smile   she _____
3 to clean   I _____
4 to close   it _____

C Add a suffix to each of these words to change it into an **adjective**.

1 fever
2 dust
3 danger
4 beauty

D Add a suffix to each of these words to change it into an **abstract noun**.

1 weary
2 dark
3 serve
4 weak

Sentences

A Change these **direct speech** sentences into **indirect speech**.

1 "I am enjoying myself," said Osman.

2 "This soup is cold!" complained Robert.

3 Have you read the newspaper?" asked Dad.

B Add capital letters and punctuation to these direct speech sentences.

1 can you get the bread said Helen and some butter

2 why does it always rain moaned Kay when I want to go out

3 one of the trees fell down cried Jan and hit the car

C Copy these sentences and underline the **main clauses**.

1 I have to hurry because I am already late.

2 Although I didn't have a coat, I wasn't cold.

3 Brush your teeth before you go to bed.

D Copy the sentences. Add **commas** where they are needed.

1 I would like some carrots turnips potatoes beans and sprouts.

2 He's wearing my jumper isn't he?

3 The gate unpainted and broken creaked in the wind.

E Join each pair of **simple sentences** to make a **compound sentence**.

1 I need to go to the doctor. I don't have time.

2 I'm sure I heard the phone. Was it the front door bell?

3 The tyre was punctured. The bumper was bent.

F Complete these as **compound sentences**.

1 I wrote a long letter _ _ _ _ _ _ _ _ _ _ _ _ _ _ _ _ _ _ .

2 She plays the piano _ _ _ _ _ _ _ _ _ _ _ _ _ _ _ _ _ _ .

3 We had a birthday party _ _ _ _ _ _ _ _ _ _ _ _ _ _ _ _ _ _ .

G Improve these sentences by using more interesting words and more detail.

1 I got a good mark in the test.

2 We had a nice day and did quite a lot.

3 "The cat got stuck up the tree," said Mandy.

H Write two **paragraphs** on one of the following subjects.

1 A School Trip   2 Sports Day   3 My House